THE SECOND

AMERICAN REVOLUTION

THE CLICK HEARD AROUND THE WORLD

Freedom, Liberty or just way too much work.

By Larry Portch

Larry Portch has co-authored several other books with his daughter Michelle about American History for children. He has always been deeply involved in investigating American History. His love of history has led him to great disconcertion of the political events of the last forty years. So it is, this led him to try to use some of his knowledge to find solutions for some of today's political problems.

Cover Designed By Stilson Greene

1

Co-Author of:

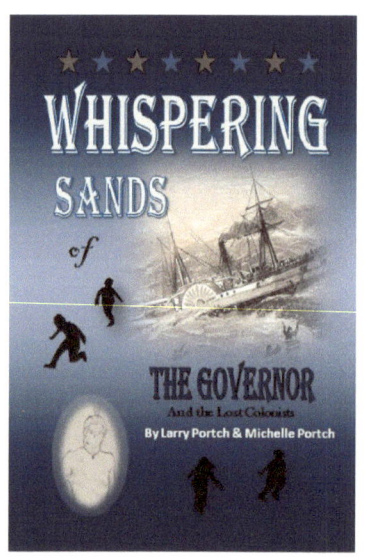 

Other books written by Larry Portch

PROLOGUE

It has been said many times that the American Revolution was about taxation without representation. As I read my history, I find the colonists had representation, but unfortunately, the King and Parliament did not agree with the colonists' view of what that representation should be. No, I believe it was taxation without proper representation. Now just fast forward 258 years, and I feel it appears we are right back to where our founding fathers were in 1776.

Ok, it's now supposedly our own government, for the people, by the people and of the people, but the majority of the colonists believe that the government of the time was their government. Henceforth, the great divide between the loyalists and those treasonous rebels, for the most part, the majority of Americans of that time - but certainly not all Americans. Many were loyal British citizens. So, I believe the great question of our day is who is to have more power, the individual, the state and then the federal government. Or is it the federal government, the state, and who the heck cares about the individual. I know that no politician is going to talk about it, that news entertainment will use it for ratings on both sides, and the main stream news will not say anything about it.

Today, polls are thrown around to support all sides of any given political issue. Help! I am so confused that I can no longer tell where the majority of the American people stand on any given issue.

I once had a teacher who told us that when it came to a debate on any given issue, that you could form a large circle and on each point of the 360 degree circumference stack 100 books in the defense of your thesis. And that when the 100 books were done, stack another 100 books, and then another 100 books, and so on and so on. On some issues, it could go for an eternity. In the end, it comes down to the acceptance of the thesis represented by each individual's brain. The amount of individual acceptance of a given thesis equals a given consensus (or the majority rules). So on any given political issue, where are the majority's points of view? And if they have them, in a republic, does it matter when you are voting for individuals that are supposed to be representing your views but are not legally bound to do so. Oh, I forgot, it is their responsibility to defend the defenseless, to protect the minority, and to make sure they get enough money, power, and media control to beat my consensus to oblivion - to change my mind or use smoke and mirrors so that my consensus appears not to be the majority's consensus. Huh? If you think you understand this, then you can surely see why I feel totally discombobulated, if not confused than just so disgusted that I do not desire to hear about one more political issue - that my vote has no power or meaning and why bother with it at all. Just leave me alone. Although, I do know that it does concern me, I just can't take it.

I remember my father's advice from when I was young. "Son," he said, "there are two things you don't discuss in public: politics and religion. It will only get you in trouble." I will say his advice did not really resonate well with me. Although, I always did try to follow his advice – up to a point. But a little war, way back when, and having to watch a power struggle between the news media and the government, made me wonder if I was not being part of the problem rather than a solution to the problem of any given political issue. But now I'm old and I have to listen to too many of the news media taking a stick jamming it into my stomach, and twisting it to see if they could get a rise out of me. As if they were stump jumpers from the 18th and 19th century.

Well, in earlier times, stump jumpers were far few and in-between, but now the news media in all its forms is in my face 24 hours a day, 7 days a week, and 365 days a year. Please, let me not forget the government who is economically, socially, politically and punitively in my life 24 hours a day, 7 days a week, 365 days a year. Yes, one could say I'm tired, and to say it plainly, I'm tired. And if you still don't get it – I'm just sick and tired of it all. So is there not a way we can end this – please. To the point of finding a way to get some reason and your view of how you would like things to be in the United States, I offer you the Straight Vote. But before I go there, I would like discuss everyone's normal day and time. You know - that thing you have none of.

When I was young, there was a job. From 5:30 AM to 8:30 PM or longer. Then there was the house, food, soccer, shopping, dance lessons, horse lessons, home repairs, car repairs, cutting the grass, school of all types – time – what time. My wife's schedule was worse than mine. Who had time to think of politics? It was the last thing on our mind, except once every four years, for the most part. After Vietnam, the government and the news media left us alone, and we just lived our lives. Oh, for the good old days, which I have to admit, did not last that long. Sound familiar to your life, either past or present? So this Straight Vote thing better be easy and simplistic. You know, how technology is making your life now, right?

Ok, so I've got a little cynical side to me. The point is that if it were fifteen to twenty years ago, we'd have no way of drastically changing our political system without major upheaval or even war. Such is not the case, today, which brings us to the Straight Vote. Are you coming to the conclusion that this book might be about something called the Straight Vote?

The Straight what?

Vote

Vote

Vote

I cannot take credit for thinking of voting on political positions and issues on your TV or computer myself. Regrettably, I am not that intelligent. I've been told who did, but he has decided to leave the political arena, if ever actually in it. And for that reason, we will leave his name out of this. If he should desire to step forward, and take credit for it, more power to him. As for myself, I have thought about it for years, and have tried to formulate a fair system that would not be too overwhelming or encumbering to a registered American voter's life. So it is, with little or further ado, I give you the Straight Vote.

THE STRAIGHT VOTE

By now, you have figured out that this is about voting by computer. One, it should be noted that we are not a democracy, we are a Republic. Two, you will not be voting on legislation or bills. Three, you will be voting on yes or no questions or multiple choice questions on issues. Four, all questions are to be simplistic. No cannot mean yes and yes cannot mean no. There are no trick questions. Five, no senator, congressman or president in a republic is responsible to vote the way the majority votes on any given issue. Six, there are to be two voting segments per year with no more than thirty questions per voting segment. Seven, the right to be allowed to vote on the system, will have very high security.

     a.   voter registration card
     b.   Photo ID
     c.   Finger Print or Eye Identification
     d.   Private Security Code
     e.   Or anything else anybody can think of

Eight, you may go back in the system and change your vote in each four month voting segment, at any time within that four months.

Nine, there are to be five monitoring stations: two inside the United States and three outside.

Ten, the second you submit your ballot, it will go to all five locations at the same time.

Eleven, anyone who votes illegally, improperly entering the system or tries to use the system to alter outcome or harm American citizens is to be charged with treason which is to be punishable by death or life imprisonment (or) war if done by outside governments or organizations.

Twelve, there will be three TV stations paid by our tax dollars: one for the Democrats, one for the Republicans, and one for educators or anyone who wants to scream and holler.

Thirteen, all national politicians, must run for national political office, only on those three stations.

Fourteen, there will be no charge for running for office on these stations. Nor any fee for registering for running for office.

Fifteen, you may vote by computer, you may vote on TV (where it is capable of being digital), you may vote by paper at your court house, library or any voting place set up by each state. You may vote by any electronical device, as long as it's capable of legally identifying you and being secure. If I missed any that you can think of, just add it to the list. Oh, you may vote by absentee ballots.

Sixteen, whatever device you vote on electronically must have photo ID and be completely secure.

Seventeen, you must be registered to vote.

Eighteen, once a given issue is settled, it cannot be brought back up for seven years. Unless, three million registered voters petition the system for a re-vote. On second vote – it stands for seven years.

Nineteen, the government is to pay outside powerful digital companies to set the system up, run it, and monitor its security and operation – not the government, but paid for by our tax dollars.

Twenty, the government of all three branches are to be handed a digital total of the voting tally of each voting segment.

Twenty-one, There is to be a board set up of twelve people to make the ballot for each voting segment's questions. Questions can come from Congress Men, senators, presidents, governors, or one hundred fifty thousand signed petitions by American citizens.

Twenty-two, it will be the job of the house and senate or total Congress to inform the American people if they have spent too much money, if the issue could cause a major problem, or do you really want to do this at all.

Twenty three, for this vote to be legally binding requires a constitutional amendment, and that can be really hard to get achieved.

Twenty-four, there are a lot of people with a lot of ideas. If I have missed some, I apologize. Email me, and I'll add it to the list.

SECURITY AND CIVIL LIBERTIES

The question of how much liberty Americans give up to how much security that should be provided by the government is a question that is hard to come to a consensus on. Before I give you a simple ballot, may I present you with a poem:

There once was a man named George
who rifled the mail of a man named Ben.
"Foul play!" screamed the men of renown.
No intolerance in our land.
"Tut tut," said the King, "I paid by the crown,
for the protection of the colonists of my land."
"No way," said the men.
"We the people are the protection of this land."
"Yeah, yeah," said the King
"I paid and paid well for the power to protect
the colonists of this land,
and now the colonists must help to repay
the cost of the crown
for the protection of which I've endowed."
"Here this," say the men,
"NOT a pence to your hand,
NO tax to indulge,
NO tyranny to endorse,
its liberty for all this land.
All men know it well,
All men know it then,
All men know it now.
LIBERTY has a high price
both then and now."

It should be known, but if not, I tell you now, this government is no better or worse than the government that the founding fathers found their selves facing in 1775. At that time, only armed revolution could force changes in government's actions. Today, due to technology, the American people have the ability to force the government to pay attention to the will of the people of this land - if we put the technology to work for us, rather than the government putting the technology to work for them. It is hard to know where Americans stand on any given issue. Think - if you were a congressman or a senator, although most are lawyers or legal conversioners for self-preservation, they have a very hard time trying to decide issues. It is constantly said that the people are split 50/50 on any given issue. That makes the congressional body, damned if they do and damned if they don't. Almost always, both sides on any given issue feel that they are doing what is best for the country. Possibly, it is time for us to let them know where we do stand. This country must have a consensus. Fifty-one percent is a majority, but I feel you will find consensus on most issues is a much higher percentage. So may I present you with a sample ballot of some of the issues for your viewing. Remember, no matter how you may disagree with others political views, that each has his right to his view. No matter how well educated or illiterate almost all of were born an American. And by the stroke of luck, each of you have the right to vote for your representative. - How about a little more power and the right to vote on issues - A little more democracy in being a Democratic Republic.

The Straight Vote Sample Ballot

| 1. Do we start to shrink the Federal Government by closing Government Agencies? | ☐ | Yes |
| | ☐ | No |

2. Which Agency do you believe we should close?	☐	The Department of Health and Human Services
	☐	The Farm Bureau
	☐	Department of Energy
	☐	Department of Education
	☐	Department of Environmental Protection
	☐	Homeland Security
	☐	Internal Revenue Service
	☐	OSCEA
	☐	Department of Interior
	☐	National Security Agency
	☐	We close no Department or Agencies of the Government

3. Should all Government Agencies not be allowed to write rules and regulations, fees, fines or randomly install taxes or rules and laws without the direct approval of the Senate and Congress of the United States?	☐ ☐	Yes No
4. Should Government Agencies be allowed to write rules and regulations and mandate taxes or fines without the approval of the Senate or Congress, or without oversight and general guidance from the Senate and Congress?	☐ ☐	Yes No
5. Should the National Health Care Act be overturned and rescinded?	☐ ☐	Yes No
6. Should we try to rewrite or change the National Health Care Act for a better outcome?	☐ ☐	Yes No

7. Should the Government take over Health Care or should we have Health Care mandated, dictated and paid for by the Federal Government sometimes known as Nationalized Medicine?	☐ ☐	Yes No
8. Should we have term limits for Senators and Congress Men?	☐ ☐	Yes No
If so, how many terms for a Senator or Congressman?	☐ ☐ ☐	2 Terms 4 Terms 6 Terms
9. If there are term limits and the Federal Government is paying their salaries, should they have a federally paid retirement?	☐ ☐	Yes No
10. Should the Federal Senate have to answer to their perspective state Governors and Senators for their decisions on votes?	☐ ☐	Yes No

11. Should the Senate of the Federal Government stay independent of its State control, if still paid by the Federal Government?	☐ ☐	Yes No
12. How much should the President of the United States be paid per year?	☐ ☐ ☐ ☐	180,000 $150,000 $100,000 $80,000
13. Should the President of the United States get paid retirement for life if he serves two terms?	☐ ☐	Yes No
14. Should the President of the United States be allowed to give direct orders to Government Agencies involving internal domestic affairs that are not involving foreign policies without the approval of the Congress and the Senate?	☐ ☐	Yes No

15. Should the President of the United States be allowed to re-allocate funding or spend money not directly approved and budgeted by the Congress or the Senate of the United States?	☐ ☐	Yes No
16. Should we start to close down Social Security?	☐ ☐	Yes No
17. Should we leave Social Security as it is?	☐ ☐	Yes No
18. If we start to close Social Security, at what age may citizens start to withdraw from having to pay for it, and must those deductions now have to go to private retirement accounts for those citizens who have withdrawn? • Age 21 and Under Stop paying at age 31	☐ ☐ ☐ ☐	Yes No Yes No

• Age 31 Stop paying at age 41 and receive ½ of Social Security Benefits	☐ ☐	Yes No
• Age 41 Stop paying at age 48; get 70% of Social Security Benefits	☐ ☐	Yes No
• Age 45 Stop paying at age 52; get 75% of Social Security Benefits	☐ ☐	Yes No
• All those above the age of 52, as of the date of legislation, must keep paying into the Social Security Systems and collect full benefits.	☐ ☐	Yes No
19. Should we raise the retirement age of Social Security?	☐ ☐	Yes No

20. To what age do we raise the retirement age of Social Security?	☐	66
	☐	68
	☐	70
	☐	72
	☐	74
	☐	75
	☐	76
21. Do we mandate that the Government put through and build the Keystone Pipeline Immediately? 22.	☐	Yes
	☐	No
23. Do we not allow the Keystone Pipeline to be built?	☐	Yes
	☐	No
24. Do we not allow any Domestic Energy of any type with the exception of coal to be exported and sold outside of the United States?	☐	Yes
	☐	No

25. Do we let coal be utilized in the United States?	☐ ☐	Yes No
26. Do we not let coal be utilized in the United States?	☐ ☐	Yes No
27. Do we reform our tax system?	☐ ☐	Yes No
28. Do we change the Federal Tax System to a straight percentage of income? 29.	☐ ☐	Yes No
30. At what percentage of income do we tax?	☐ ☐ ☐ ☐ ☐ ☐	8% 10% 14% 17% 20% 21%

31. Do we eliminate all hidden taxes such as Communication, Gas, Healthcare, Cigarette, Homeland Security or any taxes hidden in products and services passed on to consumers with no way for the people to control the taxes?	☐	Yes
	☐	No
32. Should the states get the higher bulk of taxes requiring the Federal Government to request funding from the States rather the Federal Government providing funding to the States?	☐	Yes
	☐	No
33. Do we lower corporate income tax? If so, to what percentage?	☐	Yes
	☐	No
	☐	24%
	☐	20%
	☐	16%
	☐	12%

34. Do we raise Corporate Income Tax? If so, to what percentage?	☐	26%
	☐	28%
	☐	30%
	☐	32%
35. Do we have a Federal Death Tax?	☐	Yes
	☐	No
34. Can the Federal Government keep borrowing money to fund the Government when it has spent more money than it has brought in? 35.	☐	Yes
	☐	No
37. Should the Federal Reserve be audited?	☐	Yes
	☐	No
38. Do we eliminate Corporate Income Tax?	☐	Yes
	☐	No
39. Should the Federal Reserve be closed?	☐	Yes
	☐	No

40. Should the American Economic Currency System stay on the Gross National Product support system?	☐ ☐	Yes No
41. Should we go back to the currency being supported by Gold or some rare commodity?	☐ ☐	Yes No
42. If the American people are deceived, mislead or lied to, to achieve political position or power, or to achieve their own political ideology, or a job to achieve that ideology should they be:	☐ ☐ ☐ ☐ ☐	Impeached Tried, and if proven guilty, charged with treason Lose their citizenship and be told to find another country to live in. All of the Above Left alone – it's just politics
43. If the Supreme Court holds any issue Constitutional or Unconstitutional, should it have to go back to the Congress to be upheld and not just let to die in the Judicial System as the last word?	☐ ☐	Yes No

44. Should the American people allow lobbying of any type?	☐ ☐	Yes No
45. Should we allow lobbying by individual Americans under duress or hardship by any Institution or Governmental body?	☐ ☐	Yes No
46. Should we allow no lobbying what-so-ever?	☐ ☐	Yes No
47. Do we close the borders?	☐ ☐	Yes No
48. Do we enforce existing immigration laws, and return all illegal aliens and their siblings back to their perspective homes of origin?	☐ ☐	Yes No
49. Do we give illegal immigrants a way to have legal status in the United States, but do not allow them to have citizenship?	☐ ☐	Yes No

50. Do we give existing illegal immigrants amnesty and let them have some form of working to eventually getting their citizenship if desired?	☐	Yes
	☐	No
51. How many immigrants do we allow into the country per year?	☐	25,000
	☐	50,000
	☐	75,000
	☐	100,000
	☐	200,000
	☐	300,000
52. Do we allow no immigration of any type to be allowed into the country for any reason for the next:	☐	10 Years
	☐	15 Years
	☐	20 Years
53. If any, what type of immigrants do we give precedent above others?	☐	Poor
	☐	Those of Under Political or Religious Persecution

	☐	Those that have Educational or Financial Means that would be preferred by some in the United States
	☐	No Requirements (Lottery)
54. Do we allow Federally Assisted Payments of Abortion for any reason?	☐ ☐	Yes No
55. Do we allow Federally Assisted Payments of Abortion for rape, incest or medical necessity only?	☐ ☐	Yes No
56. Do we allow Federal Funding to organizations that provide assistance of any type for abortion?	☐ ☐	Yes No
57. How much should a Federal Congressman or Senator be paid per year, knowing that the average income of the average American is only $48,000?	☐ ☐ ☐ ☐	$180,000 $150,000 $125,000 $100,000

	☐	$75,000
	☐	$50,000
58. How many staff members should a Congressman or Senator have?	☐	5 People
	☐	10 People
	☐	15 People
	☐	25 People
	☐	30 People
59. How much should an ambassador make?	☐	$180,000
	☐	$150,000
	☐	$125,000
	☐	$100,000
	☐	$75,000
	☐	$50,000

60. Do we allow drilling for oil in the United States anywhere the companies feel there is oil and under State Regulations rather than Federal?	☐ ☐	Yes No
61. Do the American People allow drilling for oil only on land approved by Regulatory Government Agencies?	☐ ☐	Yes No
62. Do we step up the speed of the government approval for permits for drilling for oil, mandating in a time lasting no longer than three months?	☐ ☐	Yes No
63. Do we allow the government to charge oil companies for lease rights on Federal Land for drilling for oil?	☐ ☐	Yes No
64. Do we allow drilling for oil or natural gas off shore?	☐ ☐	Yes No

65. Does the State or the Federal Government control drilling rights up to 75 miles off shore?	☐ ☐	Federal Government State
66. Should the Federal Government require all major oil companies having gas stations to install two natural or LP gas pumps at each of their stations within two years?	☐ ☐	Yes No
67. Should the Federal Government expedite and clear the way for new oil and natural gas piping plus refineries for both paper work and right aways with the ability to utilize roads and freeways for whatever is necessary to get the job done and at no charge?	☐ ☐	Yes No
68. Does the Federal Government keep funding renewable energy, research projects and companies?	☐ ☐	Yes No

If so, which renewable energies would you fund? (Pick one or more of the entries)	☐	Wind
	☐	Ethanol
	☐	Geothermal
	☐	Hydrogen
	☐	Nuclear
	☐	Batteries
	☐	Electric Vehicles
69. Do we allow subsidies to companies or activities other than normal tax deduction? (Normal Tax Deductions do not count as a subsidy. Privileged or Specialized Deductions are subsidies)	☐ ☐	Yes No
70. Should the congress have to go to the voters for approval of subsidies for anything or anyone?	☐ ☐	Yes No

71. Should we not allow subsidies by the Federal Government for anything or anyone?	☐ ☐	Yes No
72. Should all pieces of legislation have to stand alone with no stacking or combining of bills?	☐ ☐	Yes No
73. Should we not allow legislation or funding to be hidden in bills that are preferred or must be passed?	☐ ☐	Yes No
74. Should the Congress of the United States pass a balanced budget amendment?	☐ ☐	Yes No
75. Should the President of the United States have the ability to have a line item veto?	☐ ☐	Yes No
76. Should the American people vote on whether we go to war when not under direct attack by a foreign enemy and have the time to decide the issue?	☐ ☐	Yes No

77. Should the Congress of the United States raise the minimum wage?	☐ ☐	Yes No
78. Should the President or Congress of the United States have to take a vote of the American Citizens to increase Federal Taxes of any type?	☐ ☐	Yes No
79. Should the Federal Government or the State pay for second housing allotment for Senators and Congressional Representatives?	☐ ☐	Federal Government State
80. Should the State or the Federal Government pay for Staff Members of the Senate and Congress?	☐ ☐	Federal Government State
81. Should the Federal Government or the State pay for the salaries of the Senators and Congress Men?	☐ ☐	Federal Government State

Geesh, this is a simple ballot of 79 questions, covering a wide variety of issues. But I promise you, there are many issues, I have not listed on this ballot. As well as many issues that are going to present their selves that we do not know about yet. It should be noted that foreign affairs were not even touched on this first section of my sample ballot. It should be easy to see why Congressmen and Senators have such a hard time getting things done. Just trying to recommend issues to be settled by the American people can be staggering. Please forgive me if I missed your pet peeve. This ballot has a mere 79 questions covering 20 different issues or topics. If you broke it down to 30 questions per voting session with two voting sessions per year, it would take you a year and a half to cover the first section of our sample ballot. Now the question arises, can the Congress, the Senate and the President keep up with it. We do not want them to lose their focus on what the country has just decided. Or probably worse yet, they decide that they have no desire to give any power up and drag their feet, legislatively speaking, to cause the new voting system to fail - please, never let us not forget the talking heads or anyone who does not like how a particular issue has been settled. Even I know that this is no Panacea or even a better or fairer political system. But maybe just maybe we can get the government to finally get down to work, get things done to settle issues that have been smoldering for over forty years. It is possible, just possible, that the sixty percent of eligible voters that are not registered to vote may get it in their head that their vote now matters. Hopefully, they will take the time to push a button that could achieve some good for other Americans as well as their selves. It should be noted that in any contest there are always winners and losers. There will be many politicians that will be very unhappy when he learns that it will be very hard to become rich by being a politician in the Federal Government of the United States. That what he feels does not matter or count, and the strongest person in the United States is each individual citizen. Not lawyers, not judges, not congressmen nor senators. No, not even the President of the United States. It's just little old you and every other single voting American citizen. Just as some of our founding fathers intended, right from the start. As for me, I finally get to know where the American majority stands on any given issue. And finally, get some peace of mind.

PART II: FOREIGN AFFAIRS

Foreign Affairs, for the most part, were not covered in the first section of our sample ballot. I feel when it comes to foreign affairs, it becomes harder for the reason that it can come too fast for a cycle for the Straight Vote. But that decision is up to each individual voter and in many cases I feel the government does need some guidance on Foreign Affairs issues. So to that end, as if the first section was not long enough, I'll give you some questions which I feel need to be resolved:

The Straight Vote – Section II

80. Does the United States continue to financially support the United Nations?	☐	Yes
	☐	No
81. Does the United States reinstate troupes back into Iraq?	☐	Yes
	☐	No
82. Does the United States keep a large enough military force in Iraq – until the Iraq government is stabilized, no matter how long it takes?	☐	Yes
	☐	No

83. Does the United States give intelligence and military logistics support to Iraq?	☐ ☐	Yes No
84. Does the United States use our Air Force to support the Iraq military forces?	☐ ☐	Yes No
85. Does the United States stay out of Iraq all together?	☐ ☐	Yes No
86. Does the United States keep troops in Afghanistan for as long as it takes?	☐ ☐	Yes No
87. Does the United States Government keep forces in Afghanistan without a force agreement?	☐ ☐	Yes No
88. Does the United States Government keep forces in Afghanistan and inform the existing government that they are under United States control and military law and it will stay that way setting up a long term Marshall Plan until Alqueida and the Taliban are completely defeated and dissolved?	☐ ☐	Yes No

89. Does the United States remove all military forces from Afghanistan?	☐	Yes
	☐	No
90. Does the United States increase our military presence in North Africa?	☐	Yes
	☐	No
91. Does the United States remove all military forces from all hostile parts of the world and come home?	☐	Yes
	☐	No
92. Does the United States increase the size of the military until we can field four full standing armies, knowing we are going to have to pay for it?	☐	Yes
	☐	No
93. If the United States Army voluntary manpower does not have the ability to meet the required manpower of four full standing armies do we re-instate the draft?	☐	Yes
	☐	No
94. If we have a draft, do we draft women?	☐	Yes
	☐	No

95. Should the United States continue to use the National Guard and Reserves as our front line military force?	☐ ☐	Yes No
96. Should the United States Military National Guard and Reserves be considered in the numbers needed to fulfill the four full standing armies?	☐ ☐	Yes No
97. Do we let the CIA or the NSA collect digital data on foreign communications or listen to wired or wireless communications outside of the United States?	☐ ☐	Yes No
98. Do we let any government agency gather digital data or listen in on any type of communication in the United States without a specific court order directed at a specific individual or organization without high probable cause?	☐ ☐	Yes No

99. Do we let any company or government agency store and keep data either for themselves or for any government agency?	☐	Yes
	☐	No
100. Do we increase or decrease or eliminate the sanctions on the Iranian Government?	☐	Increase
	☐	Decrease
	☐	Eliminate
101. Do we try to negotiate with Iran over its nuclear facilities?	☐	Yes
	☐	No
102. Do we take out Iran's nuclear capabilities militarily if negotiations do not work?	☐	Yes
	☐	No
103. Do we let Iran become a nuclear power with atomic weapons?	☐	Yes
	☐	No
104. Must Eric Snowden be forced to return to the United States and stand trial for treason?	☐	Yes
	☐	No

105.	Should Eric Snowden be allowed to return to the United States with no punishment?	☐ Yes ☐ No
106.	Should Eric Snowden be allowed to return to the United States with no punishment as long as he turns over all documents and knowledge to the Congress and the Senate for a total investigation?	☐ Yes ☐ No
107.	Should the United States continue to give financial aid to governments that are hostile to the United States?	☐ Yes ☐ No
108.	Should the United States Government give financial aid to any government for any reason other than humanitarian or disaster relief?	☐ Yes ☐ No
109.	Should the United States withdraw from the world and return to more of an Isolationist Government?	☐ Yes ☐ No

110.	Should the CIA be allowed to have para military units?	☐ Yes ☐ No
111.	Should the United States military be allowed to hire private military companies for hire, either for combat, combat support, or security of any type?	☐ Yes ☐ No
112.	Should the United State Government be allowed to hire private security companies for governmental security?	☐ Yes ☐ No
113.	Should the United States State Department only use United States military for its security both on and off embassy grounds?	☐ Yes ☐ No
114.	Does the United States send and keep naval ships or aircraft carrier support groups to the China Seas in Japan?	☐ Yes ☐ No

114a. Does the United States send and keep naval ships or aircraft carrier support groups to the Eastern Pacific, Vietnam, and Australia?	☐	Yes
	☐	No
114b. Does the United States send and keep naval ships or aircraft carrier support groups to the Mediterranean?	☐	Yes
	☐	No
114c. Does the United States send and keep naval ships or aircraft carrier support groups to the North Atlantic?	☐	Yes
	☐	No
114d. Does the United States send and keep naval ships or aircraft carrier support groups to Africa?	☐	Yes
	☐	No
114e. Does the United States send and keep naval ships or aircraft carrier support groups to the Middle East?	☐	Yes
	☐	No

115. Should the United States have four reserve fleets, two on the West Coast, One in the Gulf, and one on the East Coast? And have to pay for it all?	☐	Yes
	☐	No
116. If the United States Navy cannot fulfill a large enough navy to achieve task force protection of the United States, do we increase the size of the United States Navy?	☐	Yes
	☐	No

As you can see, liberty can have a high price. You will note that the second part of this ballot was much shorter than the section on domestic affairs. I could have made this section much larger, but quite frankly, I find it can be overwhelming and believe that foreign policy is in the realm of the President of the United States. But like I said, sometimes a President could use some guidance from the American people. If by any chance, you should find the Straight Vote intriguing you may go to my website at www.straightvote.com, and add your name for a request to vote electronically or by a voting system that would give guidance to the Congress and the President of the United States. If by some chance, you would like this vote legally binding, you may add your name to a list for a constitutional amendment to be able to vote by what we are now calling the Straight Vote. If you should find or have any issues you feel need settled please forward your question to my website. (I hope) The site keeps going down.

LIBERTY FOR ALL

www.ingramcontent.com/pod-product-compliance
Lightning Source LLC
Chambersburg PA
CBHW040315010626
45792CB00022B/499